RUTH BADER GINSBURG

Supreme Court Justice

Kaitlin Scirri

Cavendish Square
New York

Published in 2020 by Cavendish Square Publishing, LLC
243 5th Avenue, Suite 136, New York, NY 10016

First Edition

Website: cavendishsq.com

Library of Congress Cataloging-in-Publication Data

Names: Scirri, Kaitlin, author.
Title: Ruth Bader Ginsburg : Supreme Court justice / Kaitlin Scirri.
Description: New York : Cavendish Square, 2020. | Series: Barrier-breaker bios | Includes bibliographical references and index.
Identifiers: LCCN 2019014845 (print) | LCCN 2019017587 (ebook) | ISBN 9781502649676 (ebook) | ISBN 9781502649669 (library bound) | ISBN 9781502649645 (pbk.) | ISBN 9781502649652 (6 pack)
Subjects: LCSH: Ginsburg, Ruth Bader--Juvenile literature. | Women judges--United States--Biography--Juvenile literature. | Jewish judges--United States--Biography--Juvenile literature. | Judges--United States--Biography--Juvenile literature. | United States. Supreme Court--Biography--Juvenile literature.
Classification: LCC KF8745.G56 (ebook) | LCC KF8745.G56 S35 2020 (print) |
DDC 347.73/2634 [B] --dc23
LC record available at https://lccn.loc.gov/2019014845

Editor: Alexis David
Copy Editor: Nathan Heidelberger
Associate Art Director: Alan Sliwinski
Designer: Christina Shults
Production Coordinator: Karol Szymczuk
Photo Research: J8 Media

The photographs in this book are used by permission and through the courtesy of:

Cover and p. 8 Chip Somodevilla/Getty Images; p. 1 and throughout jorgen mcleman/Shutterstock; p. 3 and throughout Vecteezy.com; p. 4 Ron Sachs/Consolidated News Pictures Getty Images; pp. 6, 12 Collection of the Supreme Court of the United States; p. 7AP Photo/Ed Bailey, File; p. 10 Lynn Gilbert, Own work/File: RB Ginsburg 1977 ©Lynn Gilbert.jpg/Wikimedia Commons/CCA-SA 4.0 International; p. 15 Bettmann/Getty Images; p. 16 AP Photo/Marcy Nighswander; p. 18 AP Photo/Dennis Cook; p. 20 Alex Wong/Getty Images; p. 22 PABLO MARTINEZ MONSIVAIS/AFP/Getty Images; p. 25 David Hume Kennerly/Getty Images; p. 26 TCD/Prod. DB © CNN Films - Storyville Films/Alamy Stock Photo.

Printed in the United States of America

TABLE OF CONTENTS

Ruth Bader Ginsburg, seen here in 1993, was a Supreme Court justice.

CHAPTER 1

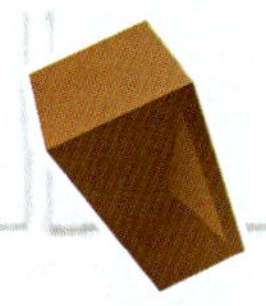
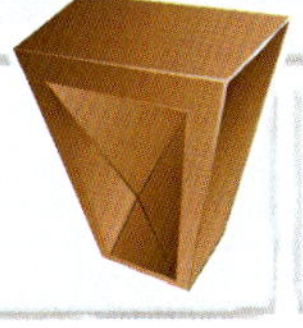
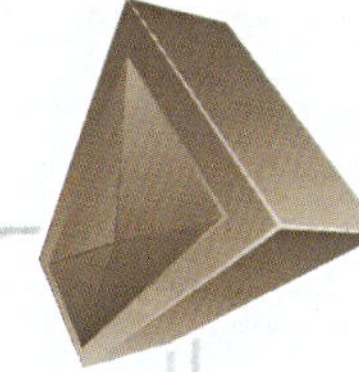

WHO WAS RUTH BADER GINSBURG?

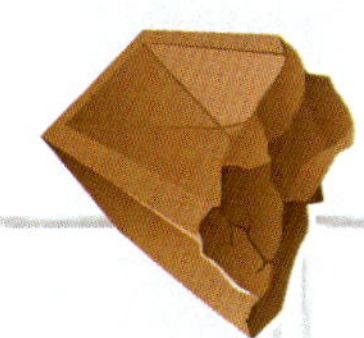

Ruth Bader Ginsburg was a Supreme Court **justice**. A justice is a judge. Sometimes people disagree with each other. They go to a court to argue. The judge listens to both sides. The judge then decides who is right. Judges must be fair. The Supreme Court is the highest court in the United States. Ginsburg became the second woman to serve on the court.

EARLY LIFE

Ruth Bader Ginsburg was born in 1933 in Brooklyn, New York. Her name was Joan Ruth Bader. In school, she had classmates also named Joan. This caused confusion, so she was called Ruth instead. The name Ruth stuck.

Ginsburg is seen here during her childhood.

EDUCATION

In the 1940s, girls had to learn sewing and cooking. There weren't many jobs they could get. Bader's

FAST FACT

Ruther Bader Ginsburg is known to many people today by just her initials, RBG.

mother disagreed with this. She took Bader to the library. Bader read books about smart and brave women. She learned that women could do many things.

Ginsburg is shown here with her husband, Martin, in 2003.

In 1950, Bader went to college. Most girls didn't go to college at that time. When she was in college, she met Martin Ginsburg. They got married. Bader's name became Ruth Bader Ginsburg. Sometimes, when women got married, they stopped studying, but Ruth Bader Ginsburg did not. She never stopped learning.

CAREER

Ginsburg wanted to help women. She wanted women to have the same rights as men. After years of school and work, Ginsburg became a judge. She protected women's rights.

In 1993, Ginsburg became a Supreme Court justice. For a long time, justices were men. Ginsburg was only the second woman to serve on the Supreme Court and the first Jewish woman to be a Supreme Court justice. She set an example for other women.

FAST FACT

When she was sick, Ginsburg wore gloves to keep germs away. She liked the gloves. Then she wore different styles.

Ginsburg can be seen here wearing stylish gloves in 2013.

PRACTICE MAKES PERFECT

Justice Ginsburg enjoyed music. She had enjoyed it since childhood. She grew up playing the piano. Ginsburg knew other students were better at playing the piano. However, she didn't give up. Instead, she worked hard to learn the piano. She took piano lessons. She practiced to improve her skills. Her hard work made her love music. She loved and appreciated music for the rest of her life.

Ginsburg studied and worked hard to become a lawyer.

CHAPTER 2

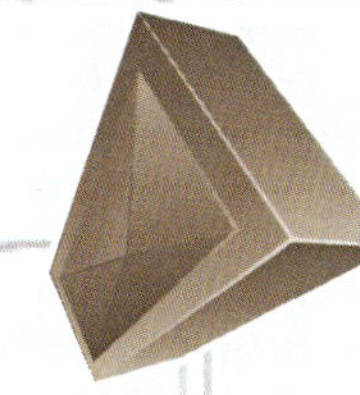

BREAKING BARRIERS

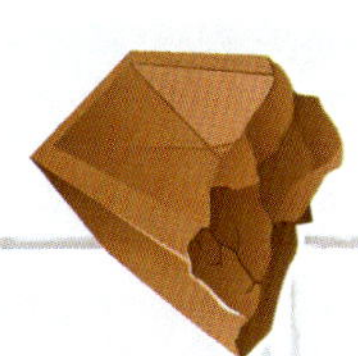

Ruth Bader Ginsburg became a wife and mother. Most wives stayed at home. Their husbands had jobs. Ginsburg wanted a job too, so she set out to get one. However, it wasn't easy.

LAW SCHOOL

After college, Ginsburg went to **law** school. She studied the law there. The law is a set of rules. Everyone must follow the law. Ginsburg wanted to be a lawyer. Lawyers argue about the law. Ginsburg

Ginsburg went to law school, even though many people would not give jobs to women.

studied very hard. She became a top student in her class.

DISCRIMINATION

It was hard for Ginsburg to find a job. Most law jobs went to men, even if women had the right skills. This was an example of **discrimination**. Ginsburg was treated differently because she was a woman. Many people thought women weren't good workers. They thought women didn't work as hard as men. Ginsburg was also Jewish. Some people didn't want to give Jewish people jobs. Ginsburg faced a lot of discrimination.

FAST FACT

While working, Ginsburg was pregnant. She wore big clothes to hide this. She was afraid of losing her job.

Ginsburg didn't give up. She finally found a job. She was a lawyer. She started breaking **barriers** for women. A barrier is something that stops someone from doing something. Being a woman made it difficult for Ginsburg to become a lawyer.

FIGHTING FOR EQUALITY

Ginsburg didn't like discrimination. She decided to fight for women's rights. Ginsburg wanted men and women to have **equality**. In 1972, Ginsburg began working on important projects to help women. She protected women's right to work. She helped women get more money for their work. Ginsburg argued many cases in favor of equality. She even argued before the Supreme Court.

Many women, like the women seen here in 1970, spoke out about the need for equal rights.

Ginsburg became a Supreme Court justice on August 10, 1993.

A GOOD REPUTATION

Ginsburg didn't have just one job. She had several. Ginsburg was a lawyer. She was also a professor. A professor is a teacher for college students. She taught the law to others. In 1972, Ginsburg became the first permanent female teacher at an important law school. Permanent means that she couldn't lose her job. Many people learned about Ginsburg. She built a good **reputation**. She was very smart. She was known as a hard worker.

FAST FACT

Ginsburg loved the opera. She appeared on stage in an opera in 2016. She spoke, but she did not sing.

FIGHTING FOR CHANGE

Ginsburg, shown here in 1985 with her husband and children, worked while raising a family.

Ginsburg and many other women experienced discrimination. Sometimes women didn't get jobs because they were women. Sometimes women lost their jobs if they had a baby. Ginsburg was treated differently than men in law school. She was told she didn't belong there. Ginsburg was also asked to take little pay for her work. Her husband already had a job, so her boss thought she didn't need money of her own.

These experiences were difficult. They inspired Ginsburg to fight for equality. She knew she wasn't the only woman who'd faced discrimination at work.

BECOMING A JUDGE

In 1980, Ginsburg became a judge. President Jimmy Carter gave her the job. She was a judge for many years. She was fair and honest. In 1993, Ginsburg got a new job. President Bill Clinton made her a Supreme Court justice. Only one woman had ever become a Supreme Court justice before her. Ginsburg worked hard, and her hard work paid off. She became a role model for girls and other women. A role model is someone others can look up to. Ginsburg showed that women could be lawyers and judges too.

Ginsburg, seen here in 2018, taught others about court cases and the law.

CHAPTER 3

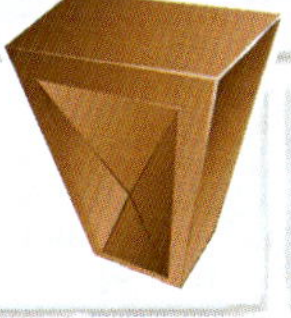
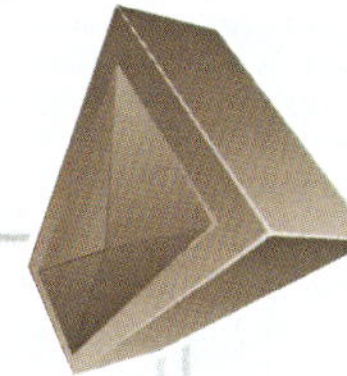

INSPIRING A NATION

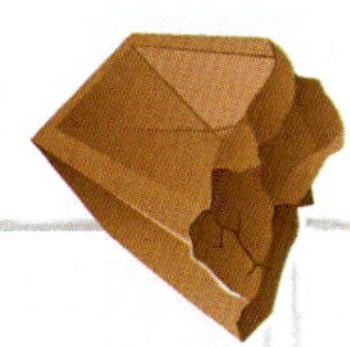

Ruth Bader Ginsburg broke barriers for women. She proved that women can be wives and mothers while working as lawyers and judges. Today, many women attend college and have jobs. This is because of the work of women like Ginsburg and they example they set.

COURT CASES

Ginsburg listened to many court cases. She had to decide what was right and wrong. She always thought for herself.

VOTES

Ginsburg voted on many court cases. She used her votes to argue for change. Some votes involved women's rights. One vote helped women attend school. Other times, she voted to help women get the health care they needed. In some cases, she argued for fair pay.

Ginsburg, shown here in 2009, worked in Washington, D.C.

AN OUTSPOKEN JUSTICE

Ruth Bader Ginsburg was outspoken. That means she wasn't afraid to say what she thought. She spoke out about court rulings that she didn't agree with. Ginsburg inspired many people. Many men, women, and groups today are working for equality. They're following Ginsburg's example.

WOMEN IN LAW

Today, a record number of women are lawyers. Ginsburg set an example for other women. She showed that women are hard workers. Women are

FAST FACT

Ginsburg participated a lot in high school. She wrote for the newspaper. She was part of the student government. She was also a baton twirler.

smart. They can work in law and other jobs. They can work in the exact same jobs as men.

WOMEN JUSTICES

Since Ginsburg became a justice, two more women have become justices. In 2009, Sonia Sotomayor became a justice. In 2010, Elena Kagan became a justice. Ginsburg's hard work opened doors for other women to follow her path.

FIGHTING BACK

Ginsburg overcame many illnesses. She fought cancer multiple times. Ginsburg took care of her health.

FAST FACT

A justice's robe has a collar. Ginsburg chose her collars carefully. Different collars showed her opinions.

WORKING TOGETHER

Sandra Day O'Connor became a Supreme Court justice in 1981. She was the first woman to become a justice. O'Connor's hard work helped make a path for Ginsburg.

Justices O'Connor and Ginsburg sit together in Washington in 2001.

O'Connor and Ginsburg were justices together. They disagreed on many issues, but they often agreed on women's rights. Together, they fought discrimination against women. A school in Virginia didn't allow women to attend. O'Connor and Ginsburg changed that. They voted that women could attend too. O'Connor and Ginsburg served together for twelve years. O'Connor left the court in 2006.

Many people liked learning about Ginsburg's workouts.

She exercised regularly. She stayed strong so she could keep working. She inspired many people to stay healthy.

Many justices **retire**. Ginsburg kept working until her death on September 18, 2020. She died of cancer. People all over the country were very sad.

Ruth Bader Ginsburg worked very hard until the end of her life. She earned her place on the court. She is still an inspiration to people everywhere.

TIMELINE

1933 Joan Ruth Bader is born in Brooklyn, New York.

1950 Bader graduates from high school and begins attending Cornell University.

1954 Bader marries Martin Ginsburg and changes her name to Ruth Bader Ginsburg.

1959 Ginsburg works as a clerk for a judge.

1980 President Jimmy Carter appoints Ginsburg as a judge in Washington, D.C.

1993 President Bill Clinton appoints Ginsburg to the Supreme Court.

2016 Ginsburg publishes her book *My Own Words*.

2020 Ginsburg dies of cancer.

GLOSSARY

barrier Something that stops someone from doing something.

discrimination The act of being treated differently from others because of a particular trait.

equality The state that occurs when all people are treated the same way and have the same rights.

justice A judge who listens to arguments in the Supreme Court and decides who is right and wrong.

law A set of rules that everyone must follow.

reputation What other people think of a person.

retire To stop working, often at an older age.

FIND OUT MORE

BOOKS

Calkhoven, Laurie. *Ruth Bader Ginsburg*. New York, NY: Simon Spotlight, 2019.

Niver, Heather Moore. *Ruth Bader Ginsburg*. New York, NY: PowerKids Press, 2017.

WEBSITE

Spotlight: The Supreme Court

https://bit.ly/2t4CpmX

VIDEO

***RBG* Documentary Trailer**

https://youtu.be/biIRlcQqmOc

INDEX

Page numbers in **boldface** refer to images. Entries in **boldface** are glossary terms.

ABOUT THE AUTHOR

Kaitlin Scirri is a freelance editor and author of books for children and teens. She holds a bachelor's degree in writing from the State University of New York at Buffalo State College. Other titles by Scirri include *Civic Values: Property Rights*, *The Science of Superpowers: Controlling Electricity and Weather*, *The Science of Superpowers: Invisibility and X-Ray Vision*, and *Inventions That Changed the World: How Facebook Changed the World*. Scirri is a long-time admirer of Justice Ginsburg and was excited to write about her accomplishments.